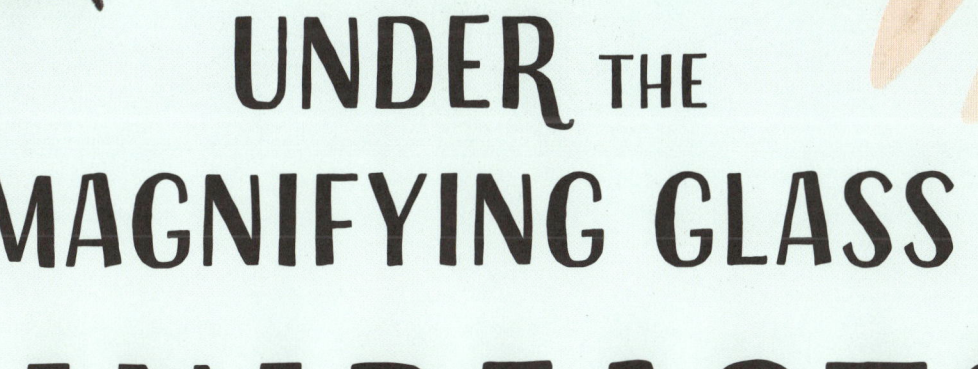

UNDER THE MAGNIFYING GLASS
MINIBEASTS

Written by ROSIE NEAVE

Illustrated by MARY ATWOOD

Consulted by CAMILLA DE LA BEDOYERE

HOW TO USE YOUR MAGNIFYING GLASS

Press out your magnifying glass and use it to look closely at the minibeasts on the pages of this book...

...then take it outside to examine tiny creatures in the wild. It's time to be a real-life wildlife detective!

Look at **MINIBEASTS** up close, and use the scale on the handle to measure them.

You can look at **PLANTS** with your lens, too. If a plant has flowers, can you see any pollen? Are the petals soft or shiny? What shape are the leaf edges?

Your lens is 3 x magnification – through it, you see things three times bigger than they really are.

If you see a **MINIBEAST** outside, observe it from a safe distance. Can you remember details so that you can draw them or make notes?

Garden snail

CONTENTS

Minibeasts are everywhere 6

BRILLIANT BEETLES 8

Up close: BUG BODIES 10

FLUTTERING BY 12

Up close: BUTTERFLY LIFECYCLES 14

WATER WORLD 16

Up close: BUG BABIES 18

FANTASTIC FLIES 20

Up close: MOVEMENT 22

BUZZING AND SCURRYING 24

Up close: HONEY HOME 26

SPECTACULAR SPIDERS 28

Up close: ATTACK AND DEFENCE 30

SCUTTLE AND SLIME 32

Up close: CAMOUFLAGE 34

Be a friend to bugs 36

Go on a bug hunt 38

MINIBEASTS ARE EVERYWHERE

What is a minibeast?

Minibeasts are small wild animals. Most of the time when people talk about minibeasts they mean any kind of insect, as well as other invertebrates (animals without backbones) such as snails, slugs, spiders and centipedes. (See page 10 for more information about invertebrates.)

Always wear SPF outside

Start your own nature journal

Will you need extra layers?

Before you go outside...

- Ask an adult to come with you, and help you plan the route – know where you are going and how to get back.
- Check the weather forecast and dress accordingly. Will you need to wear shorts, a t-shirt and sunscreen, a raincoat and boots – or something in between?
- You might want to bring a notebook and pencil for drawing and making notes, and a ruler for taking measurements. It's also a good idea to pack a drink, and a blanket to sit on while you're bug watching.

And don't forget your magnifying glass!

True bugs

Most of the time people use the word 'bug' interchangeably with 'minibeast'. But when entomologists (scientists who study insects) say 'bug', they are usually referring to true bugs: a particular kind of insect with special sucking mouthparts.

Respect nature

If you're heading outside, try not to leave any signs that you have been there. Take all your litter with you when you leave, shut gates after you, and don't damage or disturb wildlife. Share what you've learnt through drawings, photos – or by telling people!

Don't get too close!

Minibeasts may be small, but they are still wild animals. They have ways to defend themselves against danger, and they might see you as a threat. Some insects can sting or bite, so don't get close or touch them without help from a grown-up.

These panels provide ideas for where you might see the type of animal talked about on the page.

HOW TO USE YOUR BOOK

Find the tiny answers to the questions on these panels.

Use your magnifying glass to read the answers!

Use your magnifying glass to examine the details in these panels.

Are you ready? Then let's explore!

BRILLIANT BEETLES

Scarlet lily beetle
Look at the DIMPLES on the wingcases.

Striped willow leaf beetle
What COLOURS can you see on the legs?

Seven-spot ladybird
Can you spot the tiny CLAWS on its feet?

Stag beetle
Examine this beetle's JAWS. Do they remind you of antlers?

Longhorn beetle
Get up close to this beetle's super-long ANTENNAE.

Watch closely as a beetle takes flight.

You will see its elytra (hard outer wings) move apart to reveal its more delicate flying wings. Then, as it lifts off into the sky, you may hear a buzzing whirr. As it lands, a twitch of its antennae provides the beetle with vital information – is there food, or perhaps another animal, nearby?

A beetle you spot in your garden is just one of a dizzying number – about one quarter of all species alive on Earth today are beetles. Feather-winged beetles are so tiny you can barely see them, while titan beetles have bodies longer than your hand. Take a closer look at this selection of brilliant beetles.

ANSWER:
Sexton beetles bury dead animals, such as mice, underground. The females lay their eggs inside the dead animal, and when the larvae (young) hatch out, they eat it. Yuck!

UP CLOSE: BUG BODIES

Insects are invertebrates, which means they don't have backbones – or any bones at all.

Your bones together are called your skeleton, and it's what gives your body its shape and structure. Insects have an exoskeleton (hard outer covering) instead. All insects have three pairs of jointed legs, one pair of antennae (feelers), and nearly all have one or two pairs of wings.

Jewel beetle

ANSWER:
The word 'iridescent' refers to a thing that seems to change colour depending on where you view it from – like a soap bubble.

This brightly coloured jewel beetle has unfurled its flight wings from their protective cases, ready for take-off.

What do we mean when we describe a jewel beetle's colours as 'iridescent'? Find the answer!

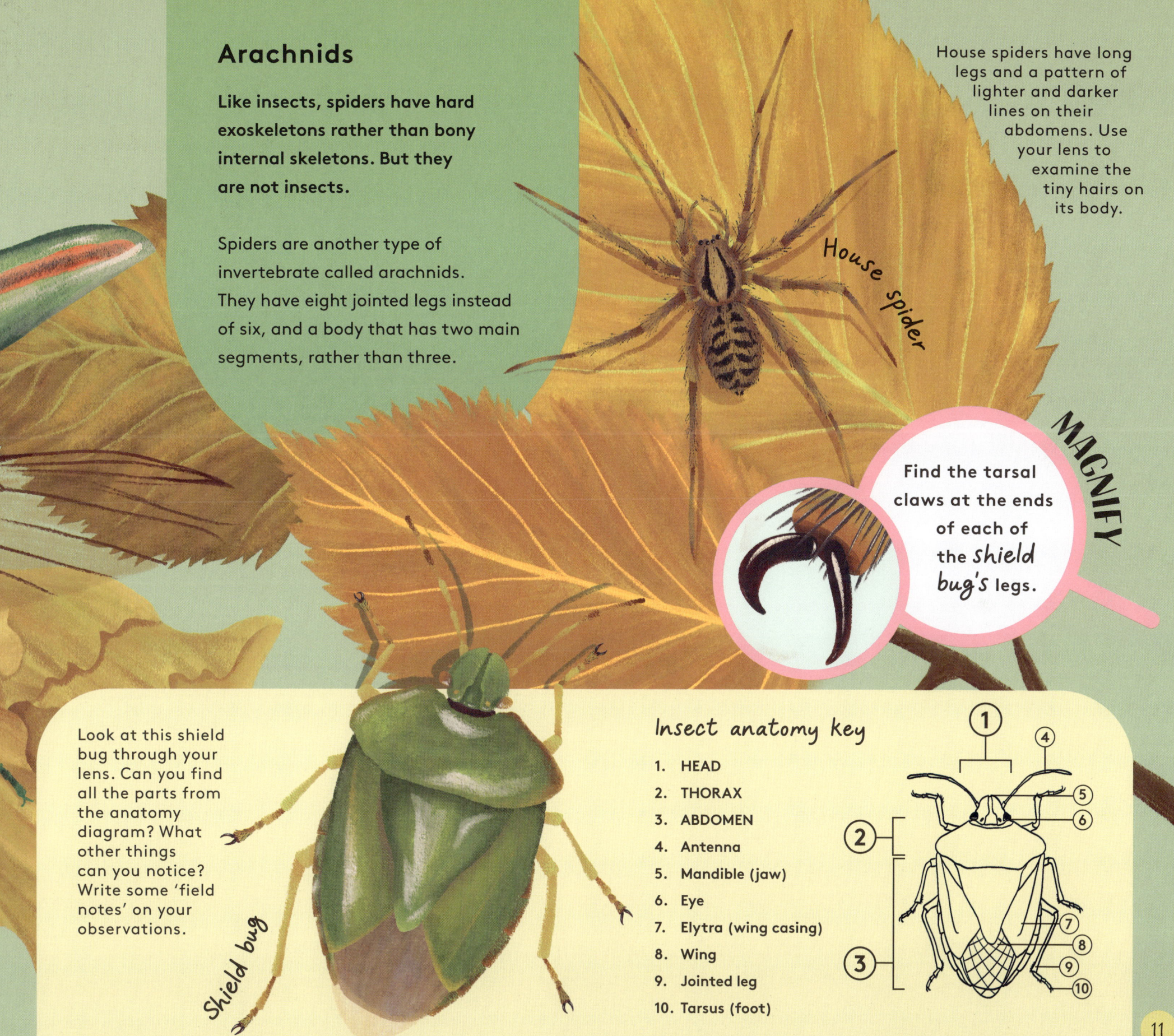

Arachnids

Like insects, spiders have hard exoskeletons rather than bony internal skeletons. But they are not insects.

Spiders are another type of invertebrate called arachnids. They have eight jointed legs instead of six, and a body that has two main segments, rather than three.

House spiders have long legs and a pattern of lighter and darker lines on their abdomens. Use your lens to examine the tiny hairs on its body.

House spider

MAGNIFY

Find the tarsal claws at the ends of each of the *shield bug's* legs.

Look at this shield bug through your lens. Can you find all the parts from the anatomy diagram? What other things can you notice? Write some 'field notes' on your observations.

Shield bug

Insect anatomy key

1. HEAD
2. THORAX
3. ABDOMEN
4. Antenna
5. Mandible (jaw)
6. Eye
7. Elytra (wing casing)
8. Wing
9. Jointed leg
10. Tarsus (foot)

UP CLOSE: BUTTERFLY LIFECYCLES

The beautiful butterflies that flit around your garden all started life as wriggly caterpillars.

A butterfly's lifecycle has four stages. Females lay eggs on plants. When a caterpillar hatches, it immediately begins to feed on the plant. Once the caterpillar is fully grown it spins a chrysalis and disappears inside it. The adult emerges as a butterfly, looking very different. This process is called metamorphosis.

2. After a few weeks, the eggs hatch. The larvae, called caterpillars, emerge and start to feed on the leaves they have hatched on.

Swallowtail caterpillar

Swallowtail eggs

1. An adult butterfly lays eggs on leaves. Many species will only lay their eggs on one particular type of plant. These are the eggs of the swallowtail butterfly.

Swallowtail chrysalis

3. When a caterpillar is big enough, it builds a chrysalis. This is called the pupal stage. Can you spot the silk 'belt' that keeps the chrysalis secure? Inside, metamorphosis takes weeks, and sometimes months.

How do swallowtail caterpillars defend themselves? Find the answer!

MAGNIFY

Look closely at the scales on the *butterfly's* wings.

4. When it is fully formed, the butterfly emerges. At first its wings are damp and crumpled. It has to wait a little while before it is ready to fly.

The adult stage of an insect's lifecycle is known as the imago.

Adult swallowtail

Butterfly lifecycle

Egg — Caterpillar — Chrysalis — Imago

WATER WORLD

Lakes, ponds, and even puddles can teem with tiny life.

Many insects and other creepy crawlies start their lives in freshwater, and the adult forms can often be seen nearby.

Damselflies and dragonflies dart and dash above the surface. They look delicate to us, but to smaller insects they are deadly, snatching their prey from the air as they fly. On the surface you might spot pond skaters, which use water-repelling hairs on their feet to 'walk' on the top of the water. Beneath the surface lurk beetles, snails and even spiders!

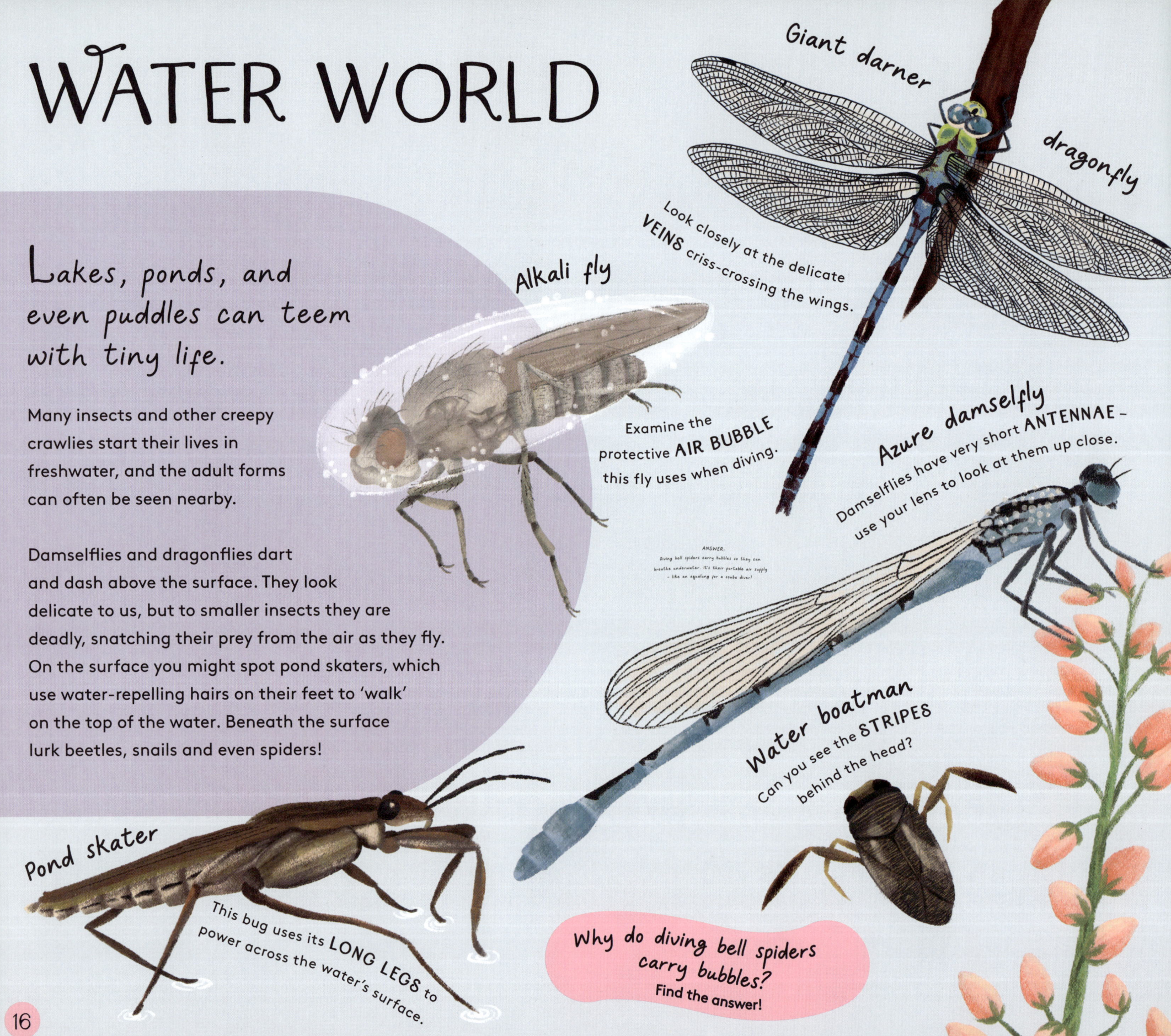

Giant darner dragonfly
Look closely at the delicate VEINS criss-crossing the wings.

Alkali fly
Examine the protective AIR BUBBLE this fly uses when diving.

Azure damselfly
Damselflies have very short ANTENNAE – use your lens to look at them up close.

Water boatman
Can you see the STRIPES behind the head?

Pond skater
This bug uses its LONG LEGS to power across the water's surface.

ANSWER:
Diving bell spiders carry bubbles so they can breathe underwater. It's their portable air supply – like an aqualung for a scuba diver!

Why do diving bell spiders carry bubbles?
Find the answer!

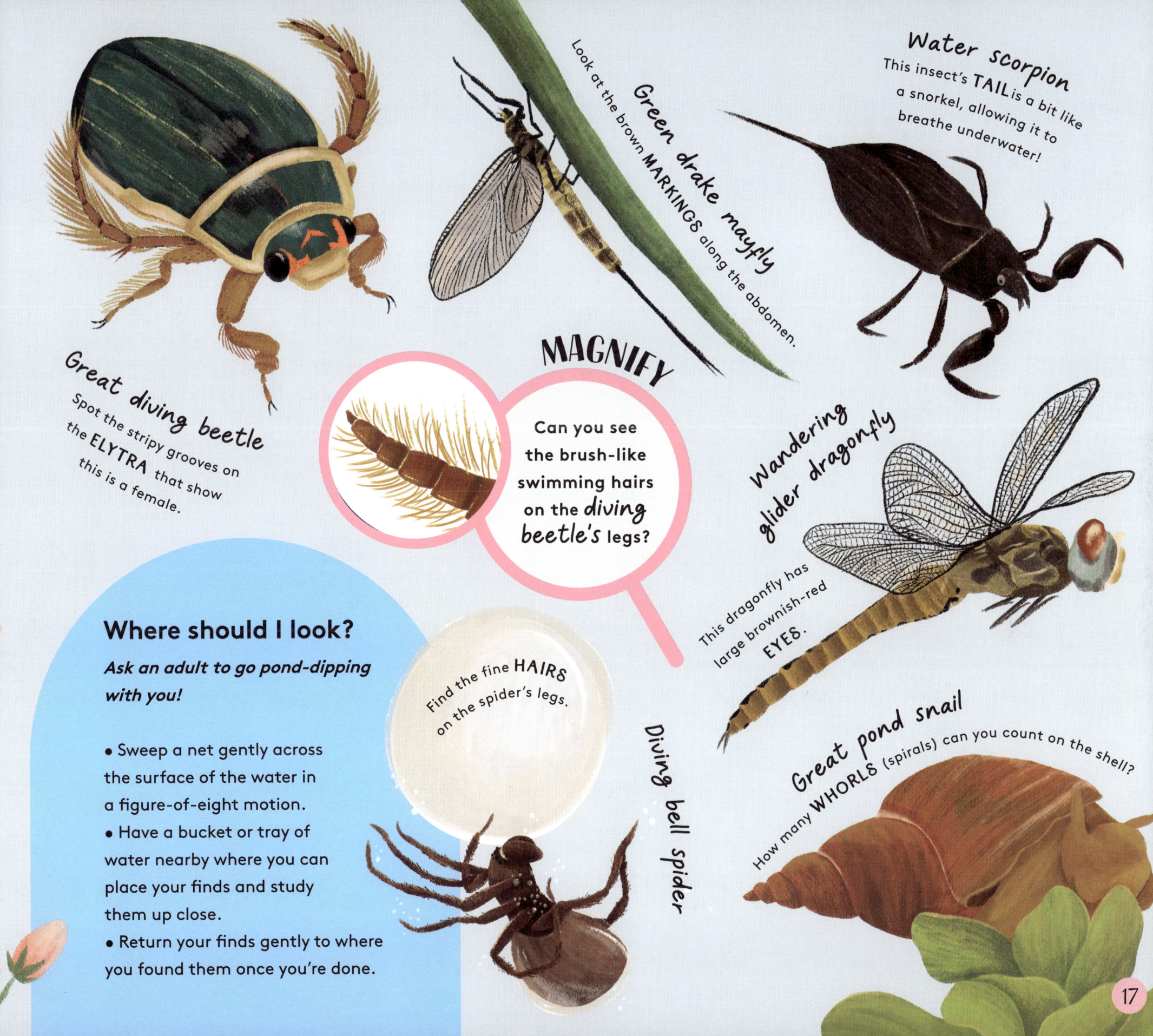

Great diving beetle Spot the stripy grooves on the ELYTRA that show this is a female.

Green drake mayfly Look at the brown MARKINGS along the abdomen.

Water scorpion This insect's TAIL is a bit like a snorkel, allowing it to breathe underwater!

MAGNIFY Can you see the brush-like swimming hairs on the **diving beetle's** legs?

Wandering glider dragonfly This dragonfly has large brownish-red EYES.

Find the fine HAIRS on the spider's legs.

Diving bell spider

Great pond snail How many WHORLS (spirals) can you count on the shell?

Where should I look?

Ask an adult to go pond-dipping with you!

- Sweep a net gently across the surface of the water in a figure-of-eight motion.
- Have a bucket or tray of water nearby where you can place your finds and study them up close.
- Return your finds gently to where you found them once you're done.

UP CLOSE: BUG BABIES

Many minibeasts besides butterflies have babies that look different to their adult forms.

These babies are called larvae or nymphs, and caterpillars are just one kind. Some insect larvae have gills and live in water. There they eat, grow, and moult (shed their outer casing). They only emerge and start to breathe air when they are ready to change into their adult forms.

3. The last moult is special, making the biggest changes to their body shape. The wings that have developed slowly unfurl.

2. When they are ready to develop into adults, dragonfly and damselfly larvae move to the surface and moult one last time.

Adult dragonfly

Adult damselfly

How long do adult cicadas live for? Find the answer!

1. Dragonfly and damselfly larvae are fierce hunters. They live underwater, eating worms, snails, and even small fish!

Dragonfly larva

Damselfly larva

Some female caddisflies release their eggs into water as they fly.

Adult caddisfly

This caddisfly larva has built its protective case using small pebbles.

MAGNIFY

Caddisfly larvae live in water and build cases to protect their bodies. When they are ready to metamorphose, the case becomes a cocoon.

Caddisfly larva

Adult mosquito

Wriggly mosquito larvae hang from the water's surface.

Mosquito larva

ANSWER: Adult cicadas live for less than two months

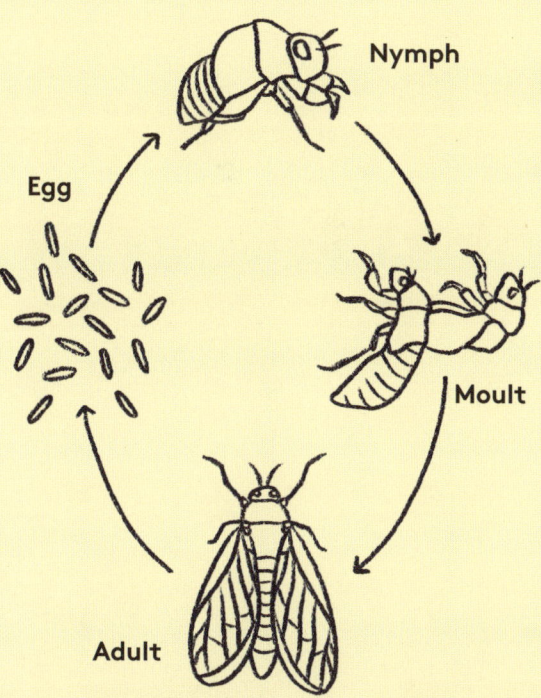

Nymphs

Larvae look very different to their parents, while nymphs look like smaller, wingless versions of their adult forms.

Cicadas hatch out of eggs above ground, and the nymphs burrow underground and live there, getting bigger and moulting (shedding their skin) as they grow. Then they tunnel their way up to the surface, moult one last time, and emerge as adults.

Cicada lifecycle

Egg → Nymph → Moult → Adult

FANTASTIC FLIES

A fly zooming past you is a whirring buzz of wings almost too fast to follow.

Flies are known for their aerial acrobatics. Large compound eyes give flies excellent vision in the air, and clinging pads or claws on their feet allow them to land perfectly.

Flies are important pollinators, but some species can also carry a range of diseases. Certain types of mosquito spread malaria, which can be deadly to humans.

Bee fly
This fly has long, TONGUE-LIKE mouthparts.

Hoverfly
Examine the STRIPES on this fly's body.

Crane fly
The LONG LEGS of this fly help to keep it steady when flying.

Stalk-eyed fly
Use your lens to look at this fly's long EYE-STALKS.

Flesh fly
Zoom in on the silver STRIPES on this fly's thorax.

UP CLOSE: MOVEMENT

Dragonflies are one of the fastest fliers in the insect world. Common darters are named for the bursts of speed they put on when hunting their prey.

Common darter dragonfly

Minibeasts have adapted to live in almost every kind of environment on Earth, so they have lots of ways of getting around.

Like all animals, insects and creepy crawlies move to find food and escape predators. Some are good at burrowing underground, some prefer to scuttle along the surface, and many are fine fliers.

Flea

A flea pushes off with its toes and uses power from a spring inside its body to jump up to 50 times its own length into the air!

Do earthworms have eyes? Find the answer!

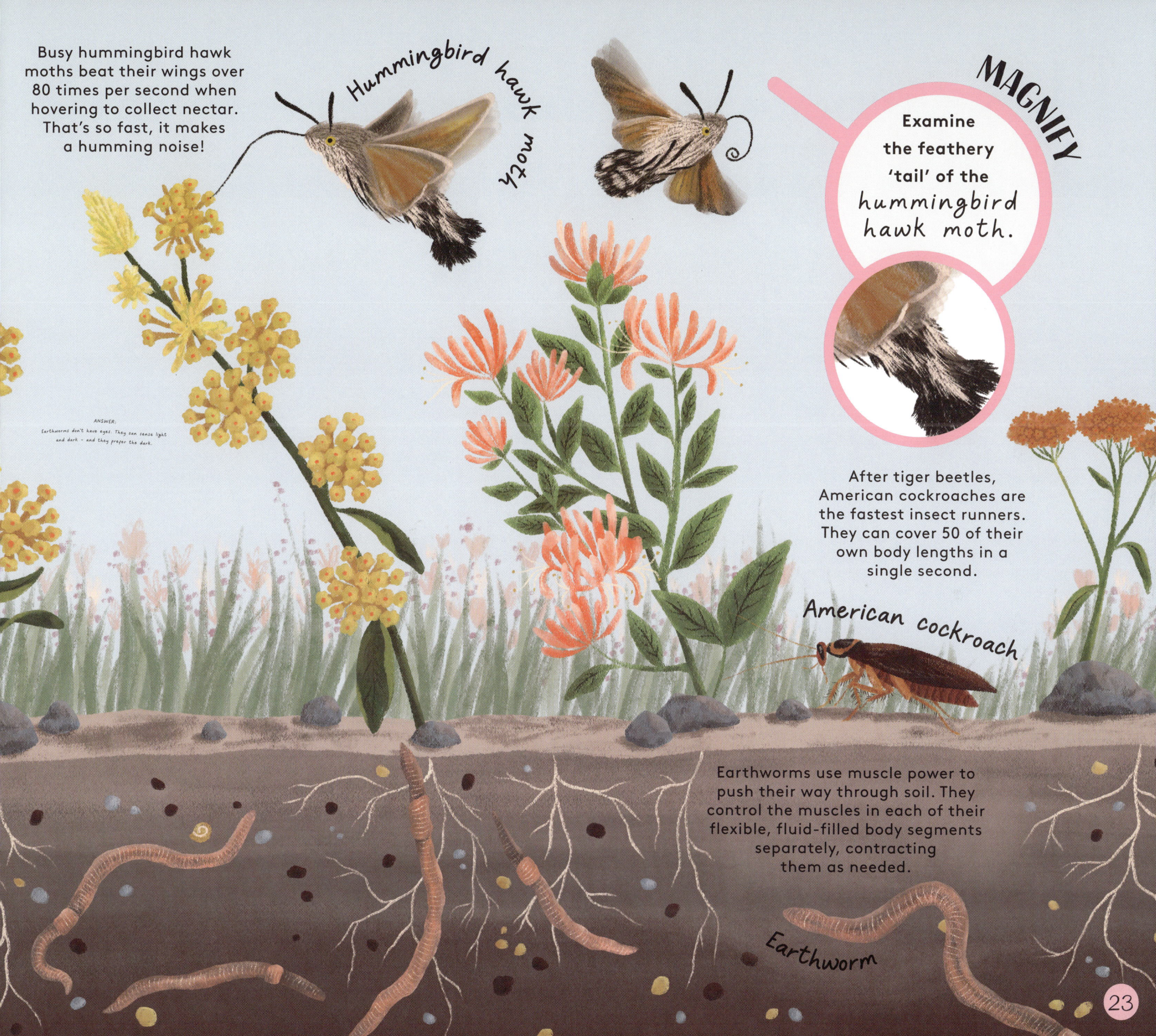

BUZZING AND SCURRYING

Velvet ant
This ant is a type of flightless WASP – can you spot the powerful sting?

Domino cuckoo bee
Use your lens to look at the many LENSES in the compound eye of this bee.

Bumblebee
Can you see the pale hairs on this BUFF-TAILED bumblebee?

Green sweat bee
Examine this bee's bright METALLIC colours up close.

Listen carefully on a warm spring day and you might hear the buzz of a bumblebee.

There are thousands of different kinds of bees, wasps and ants, which all belong to the same order of insect. Many are pollinators, helping to move pollen between flowers. This is an essential part of how many plants reproduce (make new plants). Without pollinators our world would be a much less colourful place!

Lots of species in this insect group are social, which means they live in colonies.

MAGNIFY
A bumblebee's long tongue is perfectly shaped for dipping into flowers.

Mining bee
Look closely at the brownish-orange FUR on this bee's back.

Are leafcutter bees solitary or do they live in colonies? Find the answer!

24

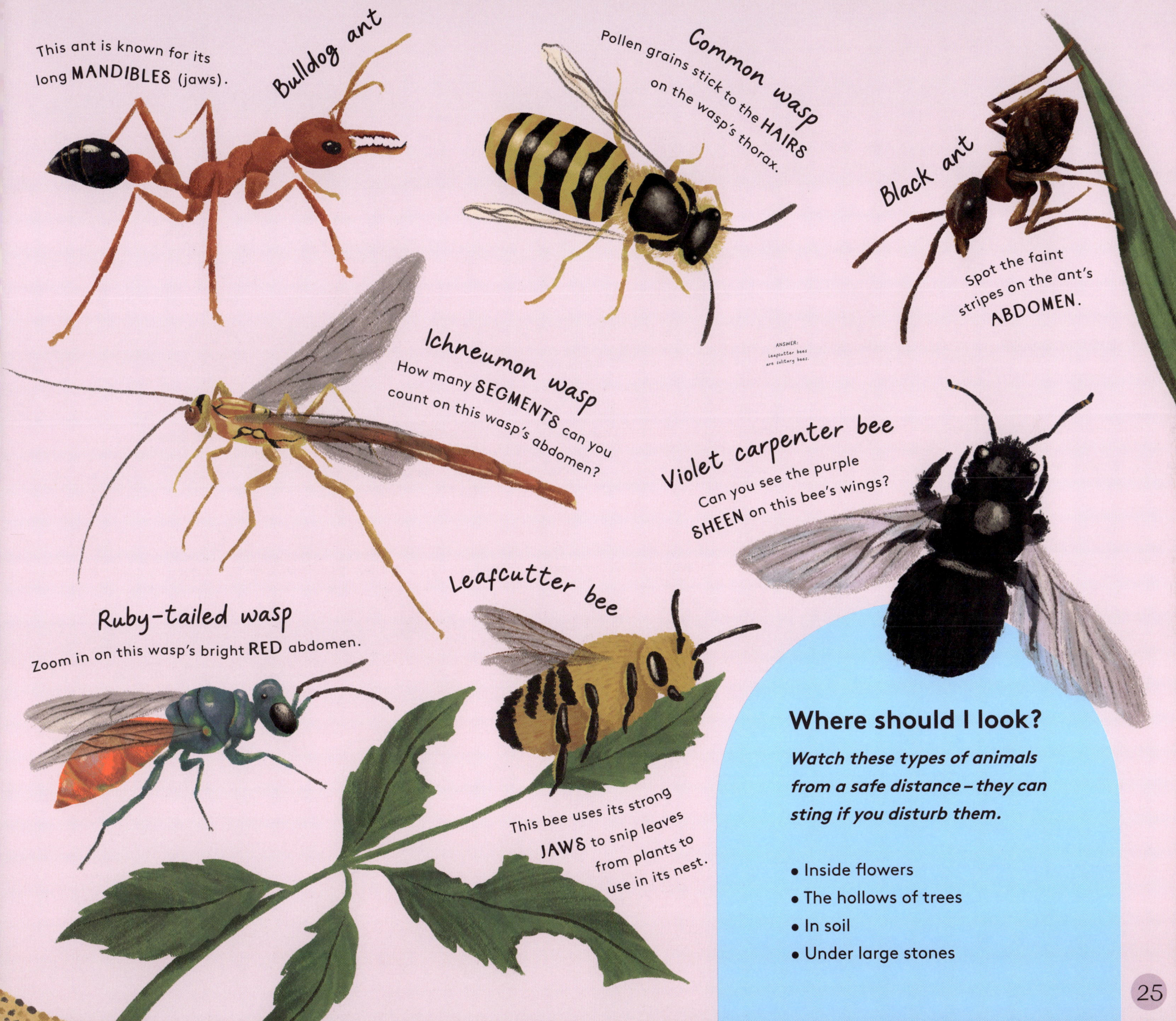

UP CLOSE: HONEY HOME

Honeybees are social insects, and all the bees in a honeybee colony live together in a nest.

A honeybee nest is made of hexagonal (six-sided) cells called 'combs', formed from beeswax – a sticky substance that the bees make inside their bodies. Inside the combs the bees store their eggs, larvae, and the food they make from pollen and nectar – honey.

The most important bee in the colony is called the queen bee. The queen is much bigger than all the other bees, and she lays all the eggs. Worker bees look after the queen and the eggs, and collect pollen from flowers. Drone bees are slightly bigger than worker bees, and their only job is to mate with the queen.

Queen bees are about twice the size of worker bees, and live for 2–3 years.

All drone bees are male, and they live for about one month.

ANSWER:
Honey badgers love to eat honey, but they eat lots of other things, too!

MAGNIFY

While a **queen bee larva** develops she is surrounded by royal jelly!

It takes around two million visits to flowers for bees to make enough honey to fill a jar.

When larvae are ready to metamorphose, worker bees cap their cells with wax. The adult bees chew their way out!

The queen bee lays her eggs inside specially chosen combs. When the larvae hatch they are fed on special jelly.

A hive may have 50,000 worker bees busy doing different tasks.

Which animal is real and loves honey – a honey badger or a honey beaver? **Find the answer!**

Waggle dance

Bees direct each other to good flower locations by dancing! The length of a bee's 'waggle dance' indicates how far away from the hive the flowers are. Its direction shows the flowers' position in relation to the position of the Sun.

Path of waggle dance

SPECTACULAR SPIDERS

Spiny orb weaver spider
How many SPINES does this spider have on its back?

Golden orb weaver spider
Look closely at the bushy black HAIRS on this spider's legs.

If a spider spots you, it will probably use its eight legs to scuttle off and hide.

A spider in your house or garden doesn't want to scare you. Most spiders are solitary, and would prefer to be left alone.

Some people think spiders look scary, but they are an important part of our ecosystem because they feed on lots of different bugs – including flies, mosquitoes, wasps, and other insects that we think of as pests. Different spider species have their own methods of catching prey, from venomous bites to sticky silk nets – and even trapdoors!

Trapdoor spider
Use you lens to see this spider's EYES – they are arranged in three rows.

Why does the flic flac spider do cartwheels?
Find the answer!

Flower crab spider
This spider's first two pairs of LEGS are extra-long – for catching prey.

Black widow spider
This spider's ABDOMEN is much bigger than the rest of its body.

Net-casting spider
Zoom in on the HEAD – it's also known as the ogre-faced spider.

28

Examine the MARKINGS on this spider's abdomen.

Garden spider

Chaco golden knee tarantula

MAGNIFY

Many *tarantulas* can flick irritating hairs at other animals to tell them to stay away.

Where should I look?

Spiders can bite if they feel threatened, so don't get too close.

Take a notebook outside so you can draw a spider web if you see one.

- Orb-weavers build wheel-like webs between larger plants
- Sheet-web spiders construct net-like webs under trees
- Funnel-web spiders make webs in corners

Wolf spider

How many JOINTS can you count on one of this spider's legs?

Use your lens to look at the spider's CHELICERAE (mouthparts).

Jumping spider
What do this spider's COLOURFUL markings look like to you?

ANSWER: Cartwheels are a speedy way for a flic flac spider to escape a predator on the hot sand of its desert home.

Ladybird spider

This spider has short hairs on its ABDOMEN – a bit like velvet.

Flic flac spider

This spider's body colour helps it to blend into its sandy DESERT home.

29

UP CLOSE: ATTACK AND DEFENCE

Praying mantids are masters of disguise. They wait on the leaves they resemble, not stirring until an unsuspecting insect strays within their reach. Then they grab it with their spiked forelegs.

Praying mantis

The world can be a dangerous place – especially if you're tiny!

Minibeasts are constantly on the hunt for their next meal – and that meal may well be another bug. Insects and arachnids have developed ingenious traps and weapons to catch each other, and equally clever ways to escape, from creating a diversion to copying more dangerous animals!

Spitting spider

Spitting spiders spit sticky, venomous silk straight onto their prey.

Antlion adults are lacy-winged flying insects, but their larvae are ferocious hunters. To catch its prey, the larva digs a pit and hides in a hole at the bottom. When a hapless insect falls in, the antlion rushes out and grabs it.

Antlion larva

How do a comet moth's tail streamers help to protect it from attack by bats? Find the answer!

Ladybirds secrete a foul-smelling and tasting liquid from their knees if a potential predator gets too close!

ANSWER:
A comet moth's tail streamers are thought to interfere with the echolocation system that a bat uses to locate its prey.

Comet moth

With a flash of eyespot markings and a flutter of tail streamers, a comet moth distracts predators so they don't know where to aim when trying to catch it.

Bombardier beetle

Bombardier beetles have an explosive reaction to potential danger. They make a deadly chemical in their abdomens, and spray it at attackers.

KEY

1. Sac containing hydroquinones
2. Sac containing hydrogen peroxide
3. Reaction chamber, where the chemicals mix
4. Explosion

MAGNIFY

Look at the feathery antennae of the *comet moth*.

SCUTTLE AND SLIME

Would you rather scurry along on more legs than you can count, or ooze slowly on a single slimy foot?

None of the minibeasts shown here are insects! Slugs and snails are gastropods – animals that slide along on one slimy foot. Centipedes and millipedes are myriapods, which have lots of legs, and bodies made up of many segments. Millipedes have two pairs of legs per segment; centipedes have one pair on each.

These animals play a vital role in our ecosystem, providing food for birds and other predators, and making our soil more nutritious for plants.

Candy cane snail
Examine the colourful STRIPES on this snail's shell.

Giant fire millipede
Look closely at the segments on the millipede's ANTENNAE.

Giant emerald pill millipede
Zoom in on the brown LINES that edge each body segment.

Common earthworm
The top part of a worm is usually darker in colour.

Common woodlouse
A woodlouse's 'armour' is lighter at the EDGES.

Leopard slug
Use your lens to look at the PATTERN on this slug.

UP CLOSE: CAMOUFLAGE

Flower mantids' camouflage allows them to hide in plain sight – so they can ambush visiting pollinators.

Sometimes the best way to stay safe is to disappear.

Some bugs have incredible camouflage, which means they look just like their surroundings. They can hide in plain sight, and other animals will find it very hard to spot them. Notice if the insects you see on your next nature walk are trying to look like their backgrounds!

Orchid mantis

ANSWER:
Orchid mantids have toothed front legs for grasping prey.

Stick insect

The bodies of some stick insects have ridges that resemble the veins on leaves.

MAGNIFY

Can you spot the *grasshopper's* ears? They are on the sides of its abdomen!

Grasshoppers are an example of simple camouflage – they are often the same colour as the plants they spend the most time on. These insects can do a sudden quick leap to escape danger.

Grasshopper

34

The markings of the peppered moth blend in against bark and lichen, helping it to hide from birds that might eat it.

Peppered moth

Leaf katydid

Leaf katydids are perfect mimics, even down to their body shape – they are almost impossible to spot.

This green and brown leaf insect is perfectly camouflaged on the leaves of its rainforest home.

Dead leaf butterfly

At rest, this butterfly holds its wings vertically, and looks just like a dried leaf.

Why do orchid mantids have teeth on their front legs? Find the answer!

Leaf insect

35

BE A FRIEND TO BUGS

Minibeasts are massively important – and they need our help.

Without bugs, lots of plants would not be pollinated, our soil would be unhealthy, and many bigger animals would go without food. The main threat to insects and other creepy crawlies is habitat loss. They need safe, healthy homes – and you can help!

ANSWER:
Insects love purple, so plants with purple flowers such as lavender and foxgloves are always popular – but a range of colours is best.

A few weeds can be wonderful

Insects don't need a perfectly mown lawn – in fact, they love the low-growing flowering plants (which we often call 'weeds') that people usually try to remove! Try choosing an area of lawn to let grow without mowing for a month. Compare the bugs you spot here to the ones you see on the mown bit. Which has more?

Ivy

Lavender

Red admiral butterfly

Fritillary butterfly

Stay away from spray!

Most weedkilling sprays are harmful to bugs and other wild animals. The best plants for your garden are ones that grow well in your soil and conditions, and don't need lots of looking after.

Foxglove

What is an insect's favourite colour? Find the answer!

Honeysuckle

Bumblebee

Frog

Spread the word

Some people are scared of minibeasts, but they are fascinating, and vital for our planet's health. Tell people about the things you have learnt in this book, and hopefully they'll start seeing bugs as fascinating friends.

Mint

GO ON A BUG HUNT

There are more than 90 minibeasts in this book! Can you find them all?

TRUE BUGS

 Pond skater
 Shield bug
 Water boatman
 Water scorpion

BEETLES

 Seven-spot ladybird
 Cockchafer beetle
 Common sexton beetle
 Firefly
 Giraffe-necked weevil
 Tiger beetle
 Striped willow leaf beetle
 Scarlet lily beetle
 Rosemary beetle
 Longhorn beetle
 Bombardier beetle

 Stag beetle
 Jewel beetle
 Golden tortoise beetle
 Great diving beetle

BUTTERFLIES & MOTHS

 Camberwell beauty butterfly
 Clouded yellow butterfly
 Swallowtail butterfly
 Red admiral butterfly
 Large white butterfly
 Painted lady butterfly
 Monarch butterfly
 Long-tailed blue butterfly
 Owl butterfly
 Pipevine swallowtail butterfly

 Queen Alexandra's birdwing butterfly
 Peacock butterfly
 Lunar moth
 Hummingbird hawk moth
 Garden tiger moth
 Comet moth
 Darwin's hawk moth
 Io moth

FLIES

 House fly
 Hoverfly
 Bee fly
 Fruit fly
 Crane fly
 Horse fly
 Flesh fly
Mosquito